PIT BOSS Gas Griddle Cookbook for Beginners

500-Day Delicious PIT BOSS Gas Griddle Recipes to Pleasantly Surprise Your Family and Friends!

Treald Wobince

© Copyright 2021 Treald Wobince - All Rights Reserved.

In no way is it legal to reproduce, duplicate, or transmit any part of this document by either electronic means or in printed format. Recording of this publication is strictly prohibited, and any storage of this material is not allowed unless with written permission from the publisher. All rights reserved.

The information provided herein is stated to be truthful and consistent, in that any liability, regarding inattention or otherwise, by any usage or abuse of any policies, processes, or directions contained within is the solitary and complete responsibility of the recipient reader. Under no circumstances will any legal liability or blame be held against the publisher for any reparation, damages, or monetary loss due to the information herein, either directly or indirectly.

Respective authors own all copyrights not held by the publisher.

Legal Notice:

This book is copyright protected. This is only for personal use. You cannot amend, distribute, sell, use, quote or paraphrase any part of the content within this book without the consent of the author or copyright owner. Legal action will be pursued if this is breached.

Disclaimer Notice:

Please note the information contained within this document is for educational and entertainment purposes only. Every attempt has been made to provide accurate, up-to-date and reliable, complete information. No warranties of any kind are expressed or implied. Readers acknowledge that the author is not engaging in the rendering of legal, financial, medical or professional advice.

By reading this document, the reader agrees that under no circumstances are we responsible for any losses, direct or indirect, which are incurred as a result of the use of information contained within this document, including, but not limited to, errors, omissions, or inaccuracies.

Table of Contents

Introduction 6
Recipes 7
    Halibut 7
    Ahi Tuna 8
    Scallops 9
    Mango BBQ Sauce 10
    Blackberry Smoothie 11
    Healthy Green Smoothie 12
    Delicious Cinnamon Smoothie 13
    Protein Muffins 14
    Energy Booster Breakfast Smoothie 15
    Cheese Blueberry Smoothie 16
    Shrimp 17
    Tasty Berry Smoothie 18
    Coconut Avocado Smoothie 19
    Lime Ginger Salmon 20
    Cinnamon Coconut Smoothie 21
    Chocó Chia Pudding 22
    BBQ White Sauce 23
    Hibachi Salmon 24
    Coconut Kale Muffins 25
    Easy BBQ Sauce 26
    Salmon 27
    Salmon Lime Burgers 28
    Shrimp Scampi 29

Cheese Zucchini Eggplant 30

Perfect Honey BBQ Sauce 31

Chocolate Fudge 32

Healthy Waffles 33

Pumpkin Muffins 34

Peach BBQ Sauce 35

Lemon Mousse 37

Cheesy Spinach Quiche 38

Sweet & Spicy BBQ Sauce 39

Shrimp On The Barbie 40

Creamy Raspberry Smoothie 41

Chia Spinach Pancakes 42

Feta Kale Frittata 43

Choco Sunflower Butter Smoothie 44

Salmon 45

Bananas Foster 46

Quick Chocó Brownie 47

Vegetable Quiche 48

Blueberry Muffins 49

Avocado Pudding 50

Egg & Bacon French Toast Panini 51

Almond Butter Brownies 53

Swordfish 54

Cowgirl Steak & Eqas on the Griddle 55

Pesto Pistachio Shrimp 56

Chicken Fajita Omelet 57

Cheesy Stuffed Steak Rolls 59

Broccoli Nuggets 61

Cheesesteak Sloppy Joes.. 62

Seafood Stuffed Sole 63

Hibachi Chicken 64

Coconut Bread 66

Shrimp Tacos With Lime Crema 67

Ginger Avocado Kale Salad 69

Chocolate Peanut Butter Cookies 70

Simple Almond Butter Fudge 72

Raspberry Chia Pudding 73

Coconut Peanut Butter Fudge 74

Gluten Free Mashed Potato Cakes 75

Breaded Pork Chops 77

Smashed Cheeseburgers...79

Philly Cheesesteak Rolls With Puff Pastry 80

Elk Burgers 82

Cuban Pork Sandwich 83

Parmesan Crusted Smashed Potatoes 85

Conclusion..**86**

Introduction

This cookbook contains all the information about the PIT BOSS Gas Griddle from basics. How does griddle work? What kind of accessories are you using? This book brings the benefits of pit boss gas grille and some tips and tricks to make you the perfect gladiator chef. This cookbook contains healthy and delicious recipes from different categories ,such as breakfast, poultry, pork, beef, lamb, seafood, fish, side dishes, vegetables, snacks and game recipes.

Best of all, this cookbook includes a variety of simple Gas Griddle recipes, all of which use ingredients that are cheap and easy to find in supermarkets.

Recipes

Halibut

Prep Time: 5 minutes
Cook Time: 7 minutes
Servings: 4

Ingredients:

- Halibut fillets, cut about 1 inch thick
- Olive oil
- Sea salt and pepper
- Fresh grated parmesan cheese
- Fresh chopped parsley
- Fresh lemon juice

Directions:

1. Brush the halibut fillets with the olive oil and sprinkle with the salt and pepper.
2. Preheat the griddle grill to high.
3. Spray the grill with spray oil, and immediately place the halibut on the heat.
4. Grill for 2 minutes per side.
5. Turn the grill down to medium, and grill for 2 minutes per side.
6. Sprinkle the halibut with the parmesan, and grill an additional minute before removing from the heat.
7. Sprinkle the fillets with parsley and lemon juice, and let it relax for 5 minutes before serving.

Ahi Tuna

Prep Time: 5 minutes
Cook Time: 13 minutes
Servings: 2

Ingredients:

- Ahi steaks, cut about 1.5 inches thick
- Soy sauce
- Brown sugar
- Toasted sesame seeds

Directions:

1. Preheat the griddle grill to the highest setting.
2. Drizzle the soy sauce followed by the brown sugar on both sides of the ahi steaks.
3. Roll the steaks in the sesame seeds.
4. Spray the grill with spray oil.
5. Grill the ahi steaks for 2-3 minutes per side.
6. Let the steaks relax for 5 minutes.
7. Slice thin and serve. Drizzle with more soy sauce if desired.

Scallops

Prep Time: 5 minutes
Cook Time: 10 minutes
Servings: 4

Ingredients:

- Large fresh bay scallops
- Real butter, melted
- Sea salt and pepper to taste

Directions:

1. Preheat the griddle grill to high.
2. Melt the butter, and set it aside so that it is ready for later.
3. Season the scallops with salt and pepper.
4. Spray the grill with spray oil, and immediately place the scallops on the heat. Brush the tops with butter.
5. Grill for 3-4 minutes per side, brushing with the butter again after flipping. The scallops are ready to turn when they pull away easily from the grill.
6. Brush the scallops again with the butter, and grill for an additional thirty seconds per side.
7. Let the scallops relax for 5 minutes before serving.

Mango BBQ Sauce

Prep Time: 5 minutes
Cook Time: 35 minutes
Servings: 12

Ingredients:

- Brown sugar -1/2 cup.
- Ground ginger -1 tbsp.
- Smoked paprika-1 tbsp.
- Ground mustard - 1 tbsp.
- Chili flakes -2 tbsps.
- Honey -3 tbsps.
- Apple cider vinegar -3/4 cup.
- Tomato paste -6 oz.
- Mango -2 cups, chopped.
- Garlic cloves -4, chopped.
- Habanero peppers -4, diced.
- Small onion -1, chopped.
- Olive oil -1 tsp.
- Pepper & salt, to taste.

Directions:

1. Heat olive oil in a griddle over a medium heat. Add peppers and onion and sauté for 5 minutes. Add garlic and sauté for a minute. Add remaining ingredients and stir until well combined. Bring to boil. Turn heat to low and simmer for 20-30 minutes. Remove griddle from heat. Puree the sauce until smooth. Pour sauce into an air-tight container and store in the refrigerator.

Blackberry Smoothie

Prep Time: 5 minutes
Cook Time: 5 minutes
Servings: 2

Ingredients:

- 1 cup unsweetened almond milk
- 1/2 cup ice
- 1/2 tsp vanilla
- 1 tsp erythritol
- 2 oz cream cheese, softened
- 4 tbsp heavy whipping cream
- 2 oz fresh blackberries

Directions:

1. Add all ingredients into the blender and blend until smooth.
2. Serve and enjoy.

Healthy Green Smoothie

Prep Time: 5 minutes
Cook Time: 5 minutes
Servings: 2

Ingredients:

- 1 cup avocado
- 1/2 lemon, peeled
- 1 cucumber, peeled
- 1 tsp ginger, peeled
- 1/2 cup cilantro
- 1 cup baby spinach
- 1 cup of water

Directions:

1. Add all ingredients into the blender and blend until smooth.
2. Serve and enjoy.

Delicious Cinnamon Smoothie

Prep Time: 5 minutes
Cook Time: 5 minutes
Servings: 1

Ingredients:

- 1/4 cup vanilla protein powder
- 1 tbsp ground chia seeds
- 1/2 tsp cinnamon
- 1 tbsp coconut oil
- 1/2 cup water
- 1/4 cup ice
- 1/2 cup unsweetened coconut milk

Directions:

1. Add all ingredients into the blender and blend until smooth.
2. Serve and enjoy

Protein Muffins

Prep Time: 10 minutes
Cook Time: 15 minutes
Servings: 12

Ingredients:

- 8 eggs
- 2 scoop vanilla protein powder
- 8 oz cream cheese
- 4 tbsp butter, melted

Directions:

1. In a large bowl, combine together cream cheese and melted butter.
2. Add eggs and protein powder and whisk until well combined.
3. Pour batter into the greased muffin pan.
4. Bake at 350F for 25 minutes.
5. Serve and enjoy.

Energy Booster Breakfast Smoothie

Prep Time: 5 minutes

Cook Time: 5 minutes

Servings: 1

Ingredients:

- 1 cup unsweetened almond milk
- 1/2 cup ice
- 1½ tsp maca powder
- 1 tbsp almond butter
- 1 tbsp MCT oil

Directions:

1. Add all ingredients into the blender and blend until smooth.
2. Serve and enjoy.

Cheese Blueberry Smoothie

Prep Time: 5 minutes
Cook Time: 5 minutes
Servings: 1

Ingredients:

- 1 cup unsweetened almond milk
- 1/2 cup ice
- 1/4 tsp vanilla
- 5 drops liquid stevia
- 1 scoop vanilla protein powder
- 1/3 cup blueberries
- 2 oz cream cheese

Directions:

1. Add all ingredients into the blender and blend until smooth.
2. Serve and enjoy.

Shrimp

Prep Time: 20 minutes
Cook Time: 5 minutes
Servings: 1

Ingredients:

- Large raw shrimp, peeled and mud vein removed
- Olive oil
- Garlic salt to taste
- Fresh lime juice

Directions:

1. Preheat the griddle grill to high.
2. Place the shrimp on the skewers through the center in the same direction.
3. Brush with olive oil and sprinkle with garlic salt.
4. Place the skewers on the grill and cook for 2 minutes on each side or until the half toward the heat has turned pink and white.
5. Drizzle with the lime juice, and grill a few seconds per side.
6. Remove from heat and serve immediately.

Tasty Berry Smoothie

Prep Time: 5 minutes
Cook Time: 5 minutes
Servings: 4

Ingredients:

- 1/2 cup blackberries
- 2/3 cup strawberries
- 2/3 cup raspberries
- 1½ cups unsweetened almond milk
- 1/2 cup unsweetened coconut milk
- 1 tbsp heavy cream

Directions:

1. Add all ingredients into the blender and blend until smooth.
2. Serve and enjoy.

Coconut Avocado Smoothie

Prep Time: 5 minutes

Cook Time: 5 minutes

Servings: 1

Ingredients:

- 1 cup unsweetened coconut milk
- 1 tsp chia seeds
- 1 tsp lime juice
- 5 spinach leaves
- 1/2 avocado
- 1 tsp ginger

Directions:

1. Add all ingredients into the blender and blend until smooth.
2. Serve and enjoy.

Lime Ginger Salmon

Prep Time: 10 minutes

Cook Time: 10 minutes

Servings: 5

Ingredients:

- 1 teaspoon onion, finely chopped
- 1/4 teaspoon sea salt
- 1 teaspoon ginger root, fresh minced
- 1 tablespoon rice vinegar
- 1 garlic clove, minced
- 2 teaspoons sugar
- 1/8 cup lime juice
- 1 cucumber, peeled and chopped
- 1/6 cup cilantro, fresh chopped
- 1/4 teaspoon coriander, ground
- 1/4 teaspoon ground pepper

Directions:

Cinnamon Coconut Smoothie

Prep Time: 5 minutes

Cook Time: 5 minutes

Servings: 1

Ingredients:

- 1/2 tsp cinnamon
- 1 scoop vanilla protein powder
- 1 tbsp shredded coconut
- 3/4 cup unsweetened almond milk
- 1/4 cup unsweetened coconut milk

Directions:

1. Add all ingredients into the blender and blend until smooth.
2. Serve and enjoy.

Chocó Chia Pudding

Total Time: 10 minutes

Servings: 6

Ingredients:

- 2½ cups coconut milk
- 2 scoops stevia extract powder
- 6 tbsp cocoa powder
- 1/2 cup chia seeds
- 1/2 tsp vanilla extract
- 1/8 cup xylitol
- 1/8 tsp salt

Directions:

1. Add all ingredients into the blender and blend until smooth.
2. Pour mixture into the glass container and place in refrigerator.
3. Serve chilled and enjoy.

BBQ White Sauce

Prep Time: 5 minutes
Cook Time: 10 minutes
Servings: 16

Ingredients:

- Mayonnaise -1-1/2 cups.
- Horseradish -2 tsps.
- Worcestershire sauce -1 tsp.
- Brown sugar -1 tbsp.
- Spicy brown mustard -1 tbsp.
- Onion powder -1/2 tsp.
- Garlic powder -1/2 tsp.
- Apple cider vinegar -1/4 cup.
- Salt- 1 tsp.

Directions:

1. Add all ingredients into a mixing bowl and whisk until smooth. Pour sauce into an air-tight container and store in the refrigerator for up to 1 week.

Hibachi Salmon

Prep Time: 12 minutes
Cook Time: 10 minutes
Servings: 4

Ingredients:

- 2 lbs. salmon fillets
- 1/2 cup teriyaki sauce
- 1 tsp. fresh grated ginger
- 2 cloves garlic
- 1/4 cup brown sugar
- 2 tsp. black pepper
- 1 Tbsp. maple syrup

Directions:

1. Mix all the ingredients together in a covered glass bowl or resealable bag, and refrigerate for several hours to overnight.
2. Heat the griddle grill to high, and grill the salmon fillets for $3-4$ minutes per side until cooked through. Salmon should be homogeneous in color with white juice between the flakes.
3. Let rest for several minutes before serving.

Coconut Kale Muffins

Prep Time: 10 minutes
Cook Time: 30 minutes
Servings: 8

Ingredients:

- 6 eggs
- 1/2 cup unsweetened coconut milk
- 1 cup kale, chopped
- 1/4 tsp garlic powder
- 1/4 tsp paprika
- 1/4 cup green onion, chopped
- Pepper
- Salt

Directions:

1. Preheat the oven to 350F.
2. Add all ingredients into the bowl and whisk well.
3. Pour mixture into the greased muffin tray and bake in oven for 30 minutes.
4. Serve and enjoy.

Easy BBQ Sauce

Prep Time: 5 minutes

Cook Time: 15 minutes

Servings: 10

Ingredients:

- Brown sugar -1-1/2 cups.
- Onion powder -2 tsps.
- Paprika -2 tsps.
- Worcestershire sauce -1 tbsp.
- Apple cider vinegar -1/2 cup.
- Ketchup -1-1/2 cups.
- Pepper -1 tsp.
- Kosher salt -2 tsps.

Directions:

1. Add all ingredients into a small griddle and heat over a medium heat. Bring to boil. Turn heat to low and simmer for 15 minutes. Store and serve.

Salmon

Prep Time: 5 minutes
Cook Time: 15 minutes
Servings: 4

Ingredients:

- Boneless salmon fillets, scaled
- Olive oil
- Sea salt and pepper to taste

Directions:

1. Preheat the griddle grill to high.
2. Drizzle the fillets with olive oil and season with sea salt and black pepper.
3. Place on the griddle grill, and cook for 3 minutes per side.
4. Turn the grill down to medium and continue grilling for several minutes until the fillet is homogeneous in color and white is beginning to appear on top of the fillet.
5. Remove from heat, and let it rest for a few minutes before serving.

Salmon Lime Burgers

Prep Time: 10 minutes

Cook Time: 10 minutes

Servings: 2

Ingredients:

- 2 hamburger buns, sliced in half
- 1 tablespoon cilantro, fresh minced
- 1/8 teaspoon fresh ground pepper
- 1/2 lb. Salmon fillets, skinless, cubed
- 1/2 tablespoon grated lime zest
- 1/4 teaspoon sea salt, fine ground
- 1-1/2 garlic cloves, minced
- 1/2 tablespoon Dijon mustard
- 1-1/2 tablespoons shallots, finely chopped
- 1/2 tablespoon honey
- 1/2 tablespoon soy sauce

Directions:

1. Mix all of your ingredients in a mixing bowl, except the hamburger buns.
2. Make 2 burger patties that are 1/2-inch thick with this mixture.
3. Preheat your griddle grill on the medium temperature setting.
4. Once your grill is preheated, place the 2 patties on the grill.
5. Grill your patties for 5 minutes per side. Serve on warm buns and enjoy!

Shrimp Scampi

Prep Time: 10 minutes
Cook Time: 10 minutes
Servings: 3

Ingredients:

- 2 tsp blackened sriracha rub seasoning
- 1/2 tsp chili pepper flakes
- To taste, lemon wedges, for serving
- Linguine, cooked
- 1½ lbs shrimp, peeled & deveined
- 1/2 cup butter, cubed, divided
- 3 garlic cloves, minced
- 1 lemon, juice & zest
- 3 tbsp parsley, chopped
- Toasted baguette, for serving

Directions:

1. Fire up your Pit Boss griddle and preheat to medium-high flame. If using a gas or charcoal grill, set it up for medium- high heat.
2. Add half of the butter to the griddle, then sauté the garlic, Blackened Sriracha, and chili flakes for 1 minute, until fragrant.
3. Add the shrimp, turning occasionally for 2 minutes, until opaque.
4. Add the remaining butter, parsley, lemon zest and juice. Toss the shrimp to coat in lemon butter, then remove from the griddle, and transfer to a serving bowl.
5. Serve immediately, with fresh lemon wedges, and toasted baguette. Serve over linguine, spaghetti or zucchini noodles, if desired.

Cheese Zucchini Eggplant

Prep Time: 10 minutes
Cook Time: 2 hours
Servings: 8

Ingredients:

- 1 eggplant, peeled and cut in 1-inch cubes
- 1½ cup spaghetti sauce
- 1 onion, sliced
- 1 medium zucchini, cut into 1-inch pieces
- 1/2 cup parmesan cheese, shredded

Directions:

1. Add all ingredients into the crock pot and stir well.
2. Cover and cook on high for 2 hours.
3. Stir well and serve.

Perfect Honey BBQ Sauce

Prep Time: 5 minutes
Cook Time: 15 minutes
Servings: 24

Ingredients:

- Ketchup- 1 cup.
- Onion powder -1 tsp.
- Garlic powder -1 tsp.
- Smoked paprika -1 tsp.
- Honey -2 tbsps.
- Apple cider vinegar -1/4 cup.
- Brown sugar-1/2 cup.
- Black pepper – 1/2 tsp.
- Salt -1 tsp.

Directions:

1. Add all ingredients into the griddle and heat over a medium heat. Bring to boil. Turn heat to low and simmer for 15 minutes. Remove griddle from heat and let it cool completely. Pour sauce into an air-tight container and store in the refrigerator for up to 2 weeks.

Chocolate Fudge

Total Time: 10 minutes

Servings: 12

Ingredients:

- 4 oz unsweetened dark chocolate
- 3/4 cup coconut butter
- 15 drops liquid stevia
- 1 tsp vanilla extract

Directions:

1. Melt coconut butter and dark chocolate.
2. Add ingredients to the large bowl and combine well.
3. Pour mixture into a silicone loaf pan and place in refrigerator until set.
4. Cut into pieces and serve.

Healthy Waffles

Prep Time: 10 minutes
Cook Time: 10 minutes
Servings: 4

Ingredients:

- 8 drops liquid stevia
- 1/2 tsp baking soda
- 1 tbsp chia seeds
- 1/4 cup water
- 2 tbsp sunflower seed butter
- 1 tsp cinnamon
- 1 avocado, peel, pitted and mashed
- 1 tsp vanilla
- 1 tbsp lemon juice
- 3 tbsp coconut flour

Directions:

1. Preheat the waffle iron.
2. In a small bowl, add water and chia seeds and soak for 5 minutes.
3. Mash together sunflower seed butter, lemon juice, vanilla, stevia, chia mixture, and avocado.
4. Mix together cinnamon, baking soda, and coconut flour.
5. Add wet ingredients to the dry ingredients and mix well.
6. Pour waffle mixture into the hot waffle iron and cook on each side for 3-5 minutes.
7. Serve and enjoy.

Pumpkin Muffins

Prep Time: 10 minutes
Cook Time: 25 minutes
Servings: 10

Ingredients:

- 4 eggs
- 1/2 cup pumpkin puree
- 1 tsp pumpkin pie spice
- 1/2 cup almond flour
- 1 tbsp baking powder
- 1 tsp vanilla
- 1/3 cup coconut oil, melted
- 2/3 cup swerve
- 1/2 cup coconut flour
- 1/2 tsp sea salt

Directions:

1. Preheat the oven to 350F.
2. In a large bowl, stir together coconut flour, pumpkin pie spice, baking powder, swerve, almond flour, and sea salt.
3. Stir in eggs, vanilla, coconut oil, and pumpkin puree until well combined.
4. Pour batter into the greased muffin tray and bake in oven for 25 minutes.
5. Serve and enjoy.

Peach BBQ Sauce

Prep Time: 5 minutes
Cook Time: 20 minutes
Servings: 24

Ingredients:

- Ketchup -1/4 cup.
- Liquid smoke -1/4 tsp.
- Dry mustard -1/2 tsp.
- Chili powder -1 tsp.
- Dijon mustard -1 tbsp.
- Worcestershire sauce -1 tbsp.
- Balsamic vinegar -2 tbsps.
- Apple cider vinegar -1/4 cup.
- Soy sauce -1/4 cup.
- Tomato paste -2 tbsps.
- Honey -2 tbsps.
- Molasses -2 tbsps.
- Brown sugar -3/4 cup.
- Water -1-1/2 cups.
- Frozen peaches -1 lb.
- Bourbon -4 tbsps.
- Jalapeno pepper -2 tbsps., diced.
- Onion -1 cup, diced.
- Olive oil -2 tbsps.
- Black pepper -1/2 tsp.
- Kosher salt -1/2 tsp.

Directions:

1. Heat olive oil in a griddle over medium heat.

2. Add jalapeno and onion and sauté for 3-4 minutes.
3. Add bourbon and cook for 1 minute.
4. Add 1 cup water and peaches and cook for 10 minutes. Remove griddle from heat.
5. Pour pan contents into the food processor and process until smooth. Return blended mixture to the griddle long with remaining ingredients and cook over medium heat for 5 minutes.
6. Remove griddle from heat and let it cool completely. Pour sauce into an air-tight container and store in the refrigerator.

Lemon Mousse

Total Time: 10 minutes

Servings: 2

Ingredients:

- 14 oz coconut milk
- 12 drops liquid stevia
- 1/2 tsp lemon extract
- 1/4 tsp turmeric

Directions:

1. Place coconut milk can in the refrigerator for overnight. Scoop out thick cream into a mixing bowl.
2. Add remaining ingredients to the bowl and whip using a hand mixer until smooth.
3. Transfer mousse mixture to a zip-lock bag and pipe into small serving glasses. Place in refrigerator.
4. Serve chilled and enjoy.

Cheesy Spinach Quiche

Prep Time: 10 minutes
Cook Time: 7 hour
Servings: 6

Ingredients:

- 8 eggs
- 2 cups fresh spinach
- 1/2 cup feta cheese, crumbled
- 1/2 cup parmesan cheese, shredded
- 1/4 cup cheddar cheese, shredded
- 3 garlic cloves, minced
- 2 cups unsweetened almond milk
- 1/4 tsp salt

Directions:

1. In a large bowl, whisk together eggs and almond milk.
2. Add spinach, parmesan cheese, feta cheese, garlic, and salt and stir well to combine.
3. Spray crock pot with cooking spray.
4. Pour egg mixture into the crock pot.
5. Sprinkle shredded cheddar cheese over the top of egg mixture.
6. Cover and cook on low for 7 hours.

Sweet & Spicy BBQ Sauce

Prep Time: 5 minutes
Cook Time: 10 minutes
Servings: 40

Ingredients:

- Tomato sauce -3-1/2 cups.
- White pepper -1/2 tsp.
- Red pepper flakes -1 tsp.
- Ground mustard -1 tbsp.
- Onion powder -1 tbsp.
- Garlic powder -1 tbsp.
- Paprika -2 tbsps.
- Soy sauce -3 tbsps.
- Worcestershire sauce -3 tbsps.
- Molasses -1/2 cup.
- Brown sugar -1 cup.

Directions:

1. Add tomato sauce, soy sauce, Worcestershire sauce, molasses, and brown sugar to a griddle and stir well to combine.
2. Add paprika, white pepper, red pepper flakes, ground mustard, onion powder, and garlic powder and stir to combine.
3. Cook sauce over a medium heat. Bring to boil.
4. Turn heat to medium-low and simmer for 5 minutes. Remove griddle from heat and let it cool completely.
5. Pour sauce into an air-tight container and store in the refrigerator.

Shrimp On The Barbie

Prep Time: 20 minutes
Cook Time: 55 minutes
Servings: 4

Ingredients:

- 3 lbs. Large raw shrimp, peeled and deveined
- 1/2 lb. Butter, melted
- 3 cloves garlic, minced
- Zest and juice of 1 lemon
- 2 tsp. Sea salt
- 2 tsp. Black pepper
- 1/4 cup grated parmesan cheese

Directions:

1. Place the shrimp on skewers.
2. Mix the remaining ingredients together and set in a bowl.
3. Heat the griddle grill to high and grill the shrimp, brushing with the butter mixture, for 2 minutes per side until they are cooked through. They will be solid in color with white and pink tones rather than blue and gray.
4. Serve with grilled summer vegetables, grilled yellow potatoes, or grilled corn (elote).

Creamy Raspberry Smoothie

Prep Time: 5 minutes
Cook Time: 5 minutes
Servings: 2

Ingredients:

- 1 cup unsweetened almond milk
- 1/2 tsp vanilla
- 1 tbsp cream cheese, softened
- 2 tbsp swerve
- 1/4 cup fresh raspberries
- 4 tbsp heavy cream
- 1 cup ice

Directions:

1. Add all ingredients into the blender and blend until smooth and creamy.
2. Serve and enjoy.

Chia Spinach Pancakes

Prep Time: 10 minutes

Cook Time: 5 minutes

Servings: 6

Ingredients:

- 4 eggs
- 1/2 cup coconut flour
- 1 cup coconut milk
- 1/4 cup chia seeds
- 1 cup spinach, chopped
- 1 tsp baking soda
- 1/2 tsp pepper
- 1/2 tsp salt

Directions:

1. Whisk eggs in a bowl until frothy.
2. Combine together all dry ingredients and add in egg mixture and whisk until smooth. Add spinach and stir well.
3. Greased pan with butter and heat over medium heat.
4. Pour 3-4 tablespoons of batter onto the pan and make pancake.
5. Cook pancake until lightly golden brown from both the sides.
6. Serve and enjoy.

Feta Kale Frittata

Prep Time: 10 minutes
Cook Time: 2 hour 10 minutes
Servings: 8

Ingredients:

- 8 eggs, beaten
- 4 oz feta cheese, crumbled
- 6 oz bell pepper, roasted and diced
- 5 oz baby kale
- 1/4 cup green onion, sliced
- 2 tsp olive oil

Directions:

1. Heat olive oil in a pan over medium-high heat.
2. Add kale to the pan and sauté for 4-5 minutes or until softened.
3. Spray slow cooker with cooking spray.
4. Add cooked kale into the slow cooker.
5. Add green onion and bell pepper into the slow cooker.
6. Pour beaten eggs into the slow cooker and stir well to combine.
7. Sprinkle crumbled feta cheese.
8. Cook on low for 2 hours or until frittata is set.
9. Serve and enjoy.

Choco Sunflower Butter Smoothie

Prep Time: 5 minutes

Cook Time: 5 minutes

Servings: 1

Ingredients:

- 1/3 cup unsweetened coconut milk
- 1/4 cup ice
- 1/2 tsp vanilla
- 1 tsp unsweetened cocoa powder
- 2/3 cup water
- 2 tbsp sunflower seed butter

Directions:

1. Add all ingredients into the blender and blend until smooth.
2. Serve and enjoy.

Salmon

Ingredients:

- 5 (6-ounces) salmon fillets
- 1/4 teaspoon of sea salt
- 1/4 teaspoon freshly ground black pepper
- 1/6 cup ginger root, minced
- 1/2 tablespoon olive oil
- 1/2 tablespoon lime juice

Directions:

1. Begin by blending the first 11 ingredients in a blender until smooth.
2. Season your salmon fillets with olive oil, lime juice, ginger, salt and pepper.
3. Preheat your griddle grill to the medium temperature setting.
4. Once your grill is preheated, place 2 salmon fillets on the grill.
5. Grill it for 4 minutes per side.
6. Cook the remaining fillets in the same manner.
7. Serve salmon fillets with prepared sauce and enjoy!

Bananas Foster

Prep Time: 10 minutes
Cook Time: 10 minutes
Servings: 4

Ingredients:

- 1/3 cup banana nectar
- 3/4 cup brown sugar
- 1/2 tsp cinnamon, ground
- Vanilla ice cream
- 4 bananas, quartered
- 1/4 cup butter
- 1/3 cup dark rum

Directions:

1. Fire up your Pit Boss Griddle and preheat to medium heat. If using a gas or charcoal grill, preheat a cast iron skillet.
2. Place a large skillet on the griddle, then melt butter in the skillet. Whisk in brown sugar and cinnamon, stirring until sugar dissolves.
3. Add the banana nectar and bananas. Stir to coat
4. Once the bananas begin to soften and turn brown, add the rum. Stir, then ignite the sauce with a stick lighter. After the flames subside, simmer the sauce for 2 minutes.
5. Divide the bananas among 4 scoops/bowls of vanilla ice cream, then spoon the warm sauce over the top of the ice cream. Serve immediately.

Quick Chocó Brownie

Total Time: 10 minutes

Servings: 1

Ingredients:

- 1/4 cup almond milk
- 1 tbsp cocoa powder
- 1 scoop chocolate protein powder
- 1/2 tsp baking powder

Directions:

1. In a microwave-safe mug blend together baking powder, protein powder, and cocoa.
2. Add almond milk in a mug and stir well.
3. Place mug in microwave and microwave for 30 seconds.
4. Serve and enjoy.

Vegetable Quiche

Prep Time: 10 minutes
Cook Time: 30 minutes
Servings: 6

Ingredients:

- 8 eggs
- 1 onion, chopped
- 1 cup Parmesan cheese, grated
- 1 cup unsweetened coconut milk
- 1 cup tomatoes, chopped
- 1 cup zucchini, chopped
- 1 tbsp butter
- 1/2 tsp pepper
- 1 tsp salt

Directions:

1. Preheat the oven to 400F.
2. Melt butter in a pan over medium heat then add onion and sauté until onion soften.
3. Add tomatoes and zucchini to pan and sauté for 4 minutes.
4. Beat eggs with cheese, milk, pepper and salt in a bowl.
5. Pour egg mixture over vegetables and bake in oven for 30 minutes.
6. Slices and serve.

Blueberry Muffins

Prep Time: 10 minutes
Cook Time: 25 minutes
Servings: 12

Ingredients:

- 2 eggs
- 1/2 tsp vanilla
- 1/2 cup fresh blueberries
- 1 tsp baking powder
- 6 drops stevia
- 1 cup heavy cream
- 2 cups almond flour
- 1/4 cup butter, melted

Directions:

1. Preheat the oven to 350F.
2. Add eggs to the mixing bowl and whisk until well mix.
3. Add remaining ingredients to the eggs and mix well to combine.
4. Pour batter into greased muffin tray and bake in oven for 25 minutes.
5. Serve and enjoy.

Avocado Pudding

Total Time: 10 minutes

Servings: 8

Ingredients:

- 2 ripe avocados, peeled, pitted and cut into pieces
- 1 tbsp fresh lime juice
- 14 oz can coconut milk
- 80 drops of liquid stevia
- 2 tsp vanilla extract

Directions:

1. Add all ingredients into the blender and blend until smooth.
2. Serve and enjoy.

Egg & Bacon French Toast Panini

Prep Time: 10 minutes

Cook Time: 10 minutes

Servings: 2

Ingredients:

- 6 bacon slices
- 4 brioche sandwich slices, day old
- 1 tbsp cinnamon-sugar
- 1 tbsp heavy cream
- 1 tbsp salt
- 1 tbsp black pepper
- 2 tbsp butter
- 6 eggs
- 1 tbsp maple syrup

Directions:

1. Fire up your Pit Boss KC Combo Grill and preheat griddle to 375°F. If using a gas or charcoal grill, set heat to medium heat. For all other grills, preheat cast iron skillet on grill grates.
2. Place butter on griddle and spread to coat surface.
3. In a pie plate, whisk together 2 eggs, heavy cream, and maple syrup.
4. Soak both sides of bread slices in egg mixture and transfer to griddle. Cook for 2 minutes, flipping halfway until egg mixture is cooked and golden. Set aside.
5. Lay bacon on the griddle, and cook 3 minutes per side, until golden.
6. Transfer to lower right-hand corner of griddle to keep warm.
7. Crack 4 eggs on top of rendered bacon fat. Season with salt and pepper. Cook 1 minute per side, or to desired doneness.
8. Lay eggs on top of French toast, add bacon, then place the other slice of French Toast on top.

9. Transfer back to griddle for another minute to warm, sprinkle with extra cinnamon-sugar, then slice in half and serve hot.

Almond Butter Brownies

Total Time: 30 minutes

Servings: 4

Ingredients:

- 1 scoop protein powder
- 2 tbsp cocoa powder
- 1 scoop protein powder
- 2 tbsp cocoa powder

Directions:

1. Preheat the oven to 350F/176C.
2. Spray brownie tray with cooking spray.
3. Add all ingredients into the blender and blend until smooth.
4. Pour batter into the prepared dish and bake in preheated oven for 20 minutes.
5. Serve and enjoy.

Swordfish

Prep Time: 5 minutes

Cook Time: 15 minutes

Servings: 4

Ingredients:

- Swordfish fillets, cut about 1.5 inches thick
- Olive oil
- Sea salt and pepper to taste

Directions:

1. Preheat the griddle grill to high.
2. Drizzle the fillets with olive oil and season with sea salt and black pepper.
3. Place on the grill and cook for 3 minutes per side.
4. Turn the grill down to medium and continue grilling for 5 minutes per side or until the sides of the swordfish are homogeneous in color.
5. Let the fish relax for 5 minutes before serving.

Cowgirl Steak & Eqas on the Griddle

Prep Time: 10 minutes

Cook Time: 15 minutes

Servings: 2

Ingredients:

- 2, 1 lbs cowgirl ribeye steak
- 1/2 jalapeno pepper, minced
- Tt pit boss chop house steak rub
- 1 lb yukon gold potatoes
- 4 eggs
- 1 tbsp olive oil
- I scallion, sliced thin

Directions:

1. Fire up your Pit Boss griddle and preheat to medium-high flame.
2. Season steaks generously with Pit Boss Chop House Rub. Drizzle olive oil on the hot skillet, then sear steaks for 5 to 7 minutes per side, depending on thickness, for medium-rare.
3. After the final sear, quickly sear edges, then add a tablespoon or two of butter, and quickly baste the steaks, turning with tongs. Transfer steaks to a cutting board, to rest for 5 minutes.
4. Meanwhile, halve the par-boiled potatoes. Season with more Chop House Rub.
5. While steaks are resting, sear potatoes in 1 tablespoon of butter, 2 minutes per side. Add jalapeño and scallions at the end, then remove from the griddle.
6. After the first turn of the potatoes, add remaining butter and a drizzle of olive oil in the middle of the griddle. Crack 4 eggs on top. Cook for 2 minutes, or until the white is opaque, but yolk remains runny.
7. Plate sliced steak with 2 sunny-side-up eggs and potatoes.

Pesto Pistachio Shrimp

Prep Time: 40 minutes

Cook Time: 10 minutes

Servings: 4

Ingredients:

- 1-1/2 lb. Uncooked shrimp, peeled and deveined
- 2 tablespoons lemon juice
- 1/4 cup Parmesan cheese, shredded
- 1/4 teaspoon of sea salt
- 1/8 teaspoon black ground pepper
- 1/2 cup olive oil
- 1/2 cup parsley, fresh minced
- 1 garlic clove, peeled
- 1/3 cup pistachios, shelled
- 1/4 teaspoon grated lemon zest
- 3/4 cup arugula, fresh

Directions:

1. Begin by adding the olive oil, lemon zest, garlic clove, pistachios, parsley, arugula and lemon juice to a blender. Blend until smooth.
2. Add your Parmesan cheese, sea salt and pepper, then mix well.
3. Toss in your shrimp and allow to marinate in the fridge for 30 minutes.
4. Thread your shrimp onto skewers.
5. Preheat your griddle grill on the medium temperature setting.
6. Once preheated, add your skewers onto the grill and close lid.
7. Grill for 6 minutes. Rotate the skewers every 2 minutes. Cooking skewers in batches. Serve and enjoy!

Chicken Fajita Omelet

Prep Time: 30 minutes

Cook Time: 12 minutes

Servings: 4

Ingredients:

- 1 cup bell pepper, sliced thin
- 2 tbsp butter
- 8 oz chicken breast, boneless, skinless, sliced thin
- 1 tbsp heavy cream
- 1/2 lime
- 1/3 cup salsa roja
- 1 tbsp vegetable oil, divided
- To taste, blackened sriracha rub seasoning
- 1 cup cheddar jack cheese, shredded
- 6 eggs, beaten
- 1 jalapeno, minced
- 1 cup red onion, sliced thinly
- 2 tbsp sour cream

Directions:

1. Fire up your Pit Boss Griddle and preheat to medium heat. If using a gas or charcoal grill, preheat a cast iron skillet.
2. Drizzle sliced chicken breast with 1 teaspoon oil, then season with Blackened Sriracha.
3. Drizzle the remaining oil on the griddle, then add the chicken. Sauté for 2 minutes, then add the bell peppers and onions. Season with additional Blackened Sriracha and continue to sauté another 2 minutes, then deglaze with fresh squeezed lime juice. Remove mixture from the griddle, set aside.
4. Turn the griddle down to low, then whisk the eggs (3 per omelet) and heavy cream.

5. Melt 1 tablespoon of butter on the griddle. Quickly pour the eggs over the melted butter.
6. Flip the eggs, then add 1/4 cup of cheese and divide all but 1/2 cup of the reserved filling into the middle of each egg. Add additional cheese and some minced jalapeño. Fold the egg over to shape the omelet.
7. Transfer the omelet to a plate and top with additional filling, cheese, salsa, sour cream, and jalapeño. Serve warm.

Cheesy Stuffed Steak Rolls

Prep Time: 20 minutes

Cook Time: 10 minutes

Servings: 4

Ingredients:

- 40 oz cream cheese, softened
- 1¼ lbs flank steak
- Pit boss chop house steak rub
- 1/4 cup sour cream
- 1 tbsp sun dried tomatoes, minced
- 1/4 tsp fennel, ground
- 2 tbsp olive oil
- 6 slices provolone cheese, sliced
- 1 cup spinach, chopped

Directions:

1. Preheat your Pit Boss Griddle on HIGH heat.
2. Place flank steak on a cutting board and slice horizontally across, to open, without completely cutting through. Use a meat mallet to pound to even thickness, if needed.
3. Season the steak on both sides evenly with Pit Boss Chophouse Steak Rub. Set aside.
4. In a mixing bowl, use a hand mixer to combine cream cheese, sour cream, sun dried tomatoes, and fennel.
5. Spread cream cheese mixture on steak, then layer spinach and provolone. Roll steak, then tie with kitchen twine every 2 inches. Slice steak in between ties to cut into individual portions.
6. On the griddle top, carefully add oil and heat.
7. Add steak rolls and sear 5 minutes per side.

8. Remove steaks from the grill and allow to rest for 5 minutes. Serve warm.

Broccoli Nuggets

Prep Time: 10 minutes
Cook Time: 15 minutes
Servings: 4

Ingredients:

- 2 egg whites
- 2 cups broccoli florets
- 1/4 cup almond flour
- 1 cup cheddar cheese, shredded
- 1/8 tsp salt

Directions:

1. Preheat the oven to 350F.
2. Add broccoli in bowl and mash using masher.
3. Add remaining ingredients to the broccoli and mix well.
4. Drop 20 scoops onto baking tray and press lightly down.
5. Bake in preheated oven for 20 minutes.
6. Serve and enjoy.

Cheesesteak Sloppy Joes

Prep Time: 10 minutes

Cook Time: 10 minutes

Servings: 6

Ingredients:

- 1 tsp beef & brisket rub
- 2 tbsp butter
- 1 green bell pepper, chopped
- 6 hamburger buns
- 8 oz mushrooms, sliced
- 1½ tbsp worcestershire sauce
- 3/4 cup beef stock
- 1 tbsp cornstarch
- 1 lb ground beef
- 2 tbsp ketchup
- 8 oz provolone, grated
- 1 yellow onion, chopped

Directions:

1. Fire up your Pit Boss Griddle and set the right half to medium heat.
2. Add the ground beef and cook for 5 minutes, until browned. Slide to the left side of the griddle to keep warm.
3. Add the butter, onions, bell pepper, and mushrooms, and sauté for 3 minutes, then mix in the ground beef. Season with Beef & Brisket, then stir in ketchup and Worcestershire sauce.
4. In a small bowl, mix beef stock and cornstarch together, then pour over the vegetable and beef mixture. Continue stirring for 1 minute, until thickened.
5. Turn off griddle, then fold in the provolone cheese until melted. Serve warm on hamburger buns.

Seafood Stuffed Sole

Prep Time: 10 minutes

Cook Time: 14 minutes

Servings: 2

Ingredients:

- 1/4 cup shrimp, cooked, peeled and chopped
- 1 tablespoon lemon juice
- 2 tablespoons butter, melted, divided
- 3/4 cup cherry tomatoes
- 1 tablespoon chicken broth
- 1/2 can (6-ounces) crabmeat, drained
- 1/2 teaspoon parsley, fresh minced
- 1 tablespoon whipped cream cheese
- 1/2 teaspoon grated lemon zest
- 2 tablespoons breadcrumbs
- 1 teaspoon chive, minced
- 2 (6-ounces) sole fish fillets, cut from the side with gutted and cleaned
- 1/4 teaspoon black ground pepper

Directions:

Hibachi Chicken

Prep Time: 20 minutes
Cook Time: 10 minutes
Servings: 4

Ingredients:

- To taste, blackened sriracha rub seasoning
- 2 cups broccoli florets, blanched
- 1 tbsp butter, unsalted
- 1 tbsp cilantro, chopped
- 2 garlic cloves, minced (for vegetables)
- 1 tsp ginger, grated (for vegetables
- 1/2 red bell pepper, sliced thin
- 2 scallions, chopped
- 2 tbsp sesame oil, divided
- 1/4 cup tamari
- 1 tbsp vegetable oil
- For serving, yum-yum sauce
- To taste, blackened sriracha rub seasoning (for vegetables)
- 1 tbsp brown sugar
- 1½ lbs chicken breast, boneless, skinless, sliced thin
- 3 garlic cloves, minced
- 1 tsp ginger, grated
- 1/2 lime, juiced
- For serving, rice noodles, cooked
- 1 tbsp sesame oil
- 1 cup snap peas, blanched
- For serving, toasted sesame seeds
- 1 tbsp vegetable oil (for vegetables)

Directions:

1. Fire up your Pit Boss Griddle and set it to medium-high heat. When hot, add 1 tablespoon of sesame oil and vegetable oil. Immediately add the chicken and season with Blackened Sriracha. When the chicken starts to brown, flip it over to brown the other side.
2. Add the garlic, ginger, soy sauce, brown sugar, butter, and the remaining tablespoon of sesame oil and stir. Turn the heat down to medium-low and let the mixture simmer for 3 minutes, until it thickens and adheres to the chicken. Add lime juice, cilantro, and scallions, then remove the mixture from the griddle.
3. After starting the sauce for the chicken, sauté the vegetables: Add sesame oil and vegetable oil to the other side of the griddle. Quickly sauté broccoli, snap peas, and red bell pepper with garlic and ginger. Season with Blackened Sriracha. Remove from the griddle after 2 minutes.
4. Serve hibachi chicken warm with sautéed vegetables, toasted sesame seeds, rice noodles, and Yum-Yum sauce if desired.

Coconut Bread

Prep Time: 10 minutes
Cook Time: 35 minutes
Servings: 12

Ingredients:

- 6 eggs
- 1 tbsp baking powder
- 2 tbsp swerve
- 1/2 cup ground flaxseed
- 1/2 cup coconut flour
- 1/2 tsp cinnamon
- 1 tsp xanthan gum
- 1/3 cup unsweetened coconut milk
- 1/2 cup olive oil
- 1/2 tsp salt

Directions:

1. Preheat the oven to 375 F.
2. Add eggs, milk, and oil into the stand mixer and blend until combined.
3. Add remaining ingredients and blend until well mixed.
4. Pour batter in greased loaf pan.
5. Bake in oven for 40 minutes.
6. Slice and serve.

Shrimp Tacos With Lime Crema

Prep Time: 10 minutes
Cook Time: 10 minutes
Servings: 4

Ingredients:

- 1/4 cabbage, shredded
- Corn tortillas
- 1/4 cup mayonnaise
- 1/4 red bell pepper, chopped
- 1/4 cup sour cream
- 1/2 white onion, chopped
- 2 tsp cilantro, chopped
- 1/2 lime, wedges
- Pit boss blackened sriracha rub
- 1 lb shrimp, peeled & deveined
- 2 tsp vegetable oil

Directions:

1. Place shrimp In a medium bowl. Season with Pit Boss Blackened Sriracha Rub, then drizzle with vegetable oil. Toss by hand to coat well then set aside.
2. In a small mixing bowl, stir together mayonnaise, sour cream, and fresh lime juice. Season to taste with Blackened Sriracha. Set aside.
3. In a small mixing bowl, combine jalapeño, onion, red bell pepper, and cilantro. Set aside.
4. Fire up your Pit Boss Portable Griddle and preheat over medium flame. If using a grill, preheat a cast iron skillet over medium-heat.
5. Place tortillas on the griddle to warm each side, then turn off the burner below.

6. Transfer shrimp to the hot griddle, and cook for 4 to 6 minutes, tossing occasionally, until opaque. For spicier shrimp, season with additional Blackened Sriracha.
7. Assemble tacos: shredded cabbage, shrimp, pepper mixture, then drizzle with sauce. Serve warm with fresh lime wedges.

Ginger Avocado Kale Salad

Total Time: 15 minutes

Servings: 4

Ingredients:

- 1 avocado, peeled and sliced
- 1 tbsp ginger, grated
- 1/2 lb kale, chopped
- 1/4 cup parsley, chopped
- 2 fresh scallions, chopped

Directions:

1. Add all ingredients into the mixing bowl and toss well.
2. Serve and enjoy.

Chocolate Peanut Butter Cookies

Prep Time: 30 minutes
Cook Time: 12 minutes
Servings: 4

Ingredients:

- 1/2 tsp baking soda
- 1/2 cup + 1 tbsp butter, unsalted
- 2 eggs, beaten
- 1/3 cup miniature chocolate chips
- 1/4 tsp sea salt
- 1 tsp vanilla extract
- 1/2 cup brown sugar
- 1/3 cup cocoa powder, dark and unsweetened
- 1½ cups flour, all-purpose
- 2 cups peanut butter chips, divided
- 1/2 cup sugar, granulated

Directions:

1. Fire up your Pit Boss Griddle and preheat to medium-low heat. If using a gas or charcoal grill, preheat a cast iron skillet.
2. In a mixing bowl, whisk together the flour, cocoa powder, baking soda, and salt. Set aside.
3. Set a metal saucepan on the griddle, then add 1/2 cup of butter to melt. Whisk in the sugars and vanilla extract and cook for 2 minutes. Remove the pan from the griddle, and transfer contents to a large mixing bowl.
4. Slowly pour the beaten eggs into the sugar mixture, whisking constantly to temper the eggs.
5. Add the dry mixture to the wet ingredients until just combined. Fold in 1 cup of peanut butter chips and chocolate chips. Refrigerate mixture for 15 to 30 minutes.

6. Remove the dough from the refrigerator, then add an additional cup of peanut butter chips.
7. Portion dough into 16 to 18 cookie balls.
8. Melt 1 tablespoon of butter on the griddle, then transfer the cookie balls to the griddle. Press down gently on the cookies, then cook for 10 to 12 minutes, flipping halfway.
9. Transfer cookies to a cooling rack for 5 minutes before enjoying.

Simple Almond Butter Fudge

Total Time: 15 minutes

Servings: 8

Ingredients:

- 1/2 cup almond butter
- 15 drops liquid stevia
- 2½ tbsp coconut oil

Directions:

1. Combine together almond butter and coconut oil in a griddle. Gently warm until melted.
2. Add stevia and stir well.
3. Pour mixture into the candy container and place in refrigerator until set.
4. Serve and enjoy.

Raspberry Chia Pudding

Total Time: 3 hours 15 minutes

Servings: 2

Ingredients:

- 4 tbsp chia seeds
- 1 cup coconut milk
- 1/2 cup raspberries

Directions:

1. Add raspberry and coconut milk in a blender and blend until smooth.
2. Pour mixture into the Mason jar.
3. Add chia seeds in a jar and stir well.
4. Close jar tightly with lid and shake well.
5. Place in refrigerator for 3 hours.
6. Serve chilled and enjoy.

Coconut Peanut Butter Fudge

Total Time: 1 hour 15 minutes

Servings: 20

Ingredients:

- 12 oz smooth peanut butter
- 3 tbsp coconut oil
- 4 tbsp coconut cream
- 15 drops liquid stevia
- Pinch of salt

Directions:

1. Line baking tray with parchment paper.
2. Melt coconut oil in a griddle over low heat.
3. Add peanut butter, coconut cream, stevia, and salt in a griddle. Stir well.
4. Pour fudge mixture into the prepared baking tray and place in refrigerator for 1 hour.
5. Cut into pieces and serve.

Gluten Free Mashed Potato Cakes

Prep Time: 40 minutes

Cook Time: 10 minutes

Servings: 6

Ingredients:

- 1/2 cup bacon bits
- 1 Cup cheddar jack cheese, shredded
- 1/3 cup flour, gluten free
- 1 tsp pit boss hickory bacon rub
- 2 tsp spicy mustard
- 2 tbsp butter
- 1 egg, whisked
- 3 cups mashed potatoes, prepared
- 4 scallions, minced

Directions:

1. In a mixing bowl, combine mashed potatoes, bacon bits, scallions, mustard, cheddar jack cheese, and beaten egg. In a separate bowl, whisk together flour, and teaspoon of Pit Boss Hickory Bacon Rub. Incorporate dry into wet ingredients. Cover and refrigerate for 30 minutes.
2. Remove mixture from the refrigerator, then divide into 12 balls (about 2½ inches in diameter), and set on a greased sheet tray. Use the bottom of a bowl to press down each potato ball to form a 1/2 inch thick patty. Season with additional sprinkling of Hickory Bacon and set aside. Fire up your Pit Boss Platinum Series KC Combo or Pit Boss Griddle and preheat the griddle to medium-low flame. If using a gas or charcoal grill, preheat a cast iron skillet over medium-low heat.
3. Add butter and oil to griddle to melt, then place mashed potato cakes on the griddle. Cook for 2 to 3 minutes per side, until golden brown.

4. Remove from the griddle. Serve warm with sour cream, reserved bacon bits and scallions.

Breaded Pork Chops

Prep Time: 20 minutes

Cook Time: 10 minutes

Servings: 6

Ingredients:

- 2 tbsp apple cider vinegar
- 2 tbsp butter
- 2 eggs, beaten
- 1/2 tbsp horseradish
- 1/2 cup mayonnaise
- 6 pork chops, bone-in
- 1/4 cup sour cream
- 1/2 cup vegetable oil
- 1 tbsp brown sugar
- 1/8 tsp cayenne pepper
- 1/2 cup flour
- 1/2 lemon, juiced
- 1½ cup panko breadcrumbs
- 1 tbsp smoked hickory sea salt
- 1/2 tbsp stone ground mustard

Directions:

1. Place pork chops on a sheet tray, blot dry with a paper towel, then season with Smoked Hickory & Honey Sea Salt.
2. Place flour, beaten egg and bread crumbs in 3 separate bowls. Dip each pork chop in flour, then beaten egg, then breadcrumbs, then set aside.
3. Prepare the Alabama White Sauce: In a small bowl, whisk together the mayonnaise, sour cream, apple cider vinegar, brown sugar, spicy brown mustard, horseradish, lemon juice, and cayenne. Whisk until fully combined, then set aside.

4. Fire up your Pit Boss Griddle and set it to medium heat. then add the oil. When oil begins to smoke, add the butter to melt, then lay out the pork chops. Cook pork chops 2 to 3 minutes per side until golden brown and crisp. For thicker chops, add 1 minute per side.
5. Serve breaded pork chops warm with Alabama White Sauce.

Smashed Cheeseburgers

Prep Time: 10 minutes
Cook Time: 10 minutes
Servings: 4

Ingredients:

- 1/2 lb bacon, half slices
- 8 cheddar cheese, slices
- 4 hamburger buns
- Pit boss chop house steak rub
- 1 tbsp butter
- 2 lbs ground beef
- 1 jalapeno, sliced thin
- 1 yellow onion, sliced thin

Directions:

1. In a mixing bowl, add ground beef and season with Chop House. Divide into 12 meatballs.
2. Fire up your Pit Boss Griddle and heat the griddle over medium heat, then add bacon slices. Render out fat, then caramelize onion in bacon fat, plus butter.
3. Lay out burger buns to toast, then turn off the burner, keeping the buns in place to keep warm.
4. Move bacon and onions to the side to keep warm, then, place 6 meatballs in their place. Using a metal spatula or stainless steel mixing bowl, smash down each meatball to 1/4 inch thickness. Sear 1 to 2 minutes per side. Place cheese on 4 of 6 patties, then top with the other. Repeat this step with the remaining 6 meatballs.
5. Assemble each smashed burger: bottom bun, cheeseburger stack, bacon, caramelized onions, sliced jalapeño, top bun.

Philly Cheesesteak Rolls With Puff Pastry

Prep Time: 15 minutes

Cook Time: 25 minutes

Servings: 14

Ingredients:

- 4 oz american or jack cheese, shredded, divided
- To taste, chop house steak rub
- 3 oz cream cheese
- 1 tbsp flour
- 1 puff pastry sheet, thawed
- 1 tbsp vegetable oil
- 2/3 cup milk
- 2 tbsp butter
- To taste, chop house steak rub (for sauce)
- 1 egg, beaten
- 1 tbsp flour (for sauce)
- 1 lb sandwich steak, shaved/sliced thin
- 1 cup yellow onion, sliced thin

Directions:

1. Fire up your Pit Boss pellet grill on SMOKE mode and let it run with lid open for 10 minutes then preheat to 400°F. If using a gas or charcoal grill, set it up for medium-high heat. Preheat the griddle to medium flame.
2. Add oil to the griddle, then cook steak for 2 to 3 minutes, turning with a spatula. Add onions, season with Chop House and cook another minute to soften. Transfer steak and onions to a bowl, then set aside to cool.
3. Meanwhile, melt butter in a sauté pan on the griddle. Stir in flour, then cook for 1 minute. Whisk in milk, then add cream cheese, and 2 ounces of shredded cheese.

Whisk until smooth, then remove from the griddle to cool slightly. Use half of the sauce in the pastry, and the other half for serving/dipping once baked.

4. Flour your rolling surface, then set the pastry sheet on top of the flour. Roll the pastry sheet into a 10 to 12 inch square, then cut into 4 squares.

5. Spoon cheese sauce on each pastry square, then divide the steak and onion mixture among the pastries. Top each with remaining shredded cheese, brush sides with beaten egg, then fold pastries over, corner to corner. Secure the seams by pressing down with a fork. Brush the top with beaten egg, then place on a sheet tray.

6. Place the sheet tray on the grill and bake for 18 to 20 minutes, until golden. Remove from the grill, cool for 5 minutes, then cut in half and serve warm with cheese sauce.

Elk Burgers

Prep Time: 10 minutes
Cook Time: 15 minutes
Servings: 4

Ingredients:

- To taste, blackened sriracha rub seasoning
- To taste, cilantro mayonnaise
- 2 lbs ground elk
- 1 jalepeno, sliced
- 1/2 tbsp butter
- 4 pieces green leaf lettuce
- 4 hamburger buns
- 4 pickled carrots

Directions:

1. Place ground elk in a mixing bowl and season with Blackened Sriracha. Divide into 4 portions, then form into large patties.
2. Fire up your Pit Boss Griddle and preheat to medium flame. If using a gas or charcoal grill, set it up for medium heat and use a cast iron skillet.
3. Place butter on the left side of the griddle and let melt. Place buns on the left side (on melted butter), and burger patties on the right side.
4. Toast the buns, then turn off the burner, keeping the buns in place to keep warm. Cook the burgers 2 to 3 minutes per side, then remove from the griddle and allow to rest for 5 minutes.
5. Assemble burger: bottom bun, cilantro mayonnaise, lettuce, burger, pickled carrots, sliced jalapeño, cilantro mayonnaise on top bun.

Cuban Pork Sandwich

Prep Time: 10 minutes
Cook Time: 270 minutes
Servings: 4

Ingredients:

- 1 tbsp butter
- 4 ciabatta bread or torta rolls, halved
- 4 dill pickle, slice
- 1/4 cup mayonnaise
- 3½ lbs pork shoulder
- 1 tbsp vegetable oil
- 3 cups chicken stock
- 1/4 cup dijon mustard
- 1 lb ham or prosciutto
- Pit boss pulled pork rub
- 8 oz swiss cheese, sliced
- 1 white onion, sliced

Directions:

1. Fire up your Pit Boss Platinum Series KC Combo and preheat to 250°F. If using a gas or charcoal grill, set it up for low, indirect heat.
2. Generously season pork shoulder with Pulled Pork Rub, then transfer to the grill grate. Smoke for 1 hour, then flip pork and smoke for an additional hour.
3. Place onion and chicken stock in a deep cast iron skillet, or metal grill pan. Transfer the pork to the skillet, then cover with a shallow cast iron skillet, or aluminum foil. Braise for 2 hours, then increase grill temperature to 300°F, and braise for 1 more hour.

4. Remove the cover then pull pork with tongs while still on the grill. The stock will have reduced, so be sure and toss the pork in the reduced, seasoned stock and onions. Remove from the grill and set aside.
5. Preheat the griddle to medium-low flame. If using a different grill, preheat a clean cast iron skillet on medium low heat.
6. Heat butter and oil on the griddle, then toast rolls, pressing down by hand or with a metal spatula. Combine mustard and mayonnaise, then spread onto both sides of rolls. Set aside.
7. Divide pork into 4 portions, and place on the griddle, along with the sliced ham. Cook for 2 to 3 minutes, rotating ham and pork. Layer pork, ham, cheese, and pickles. Cover for 1 minute to allow cheese to melt. Return rolls to the griddle, cut each portion of filling in half, then stack 2 per prepared rolls. Press each sandwich down with the bottom of a metal spatula. Carefully flip, and press down again.
8. Remove sandwiches from the griddle and serve warm.

Parmesan Crusted Smashed Potatoes

Prep Time: 20 minutes

Cook Time: 10 minutes

Servings: 4

Ingredients:

- 3 tbsp butter, melted
- 1/4 tsp garlic, granulated
- 1 tbsp parsley, leaves
- To taste salt
- To taste cracked black pepper
- 1/3 cup parmesan cheese
- 2 lbs, yukon gold potatoes
- 2 tbsp vegetable oil

Directions:

1. Fire up your Pit Boss Platinum Series KC Combo and preheat the griddle to medium-low flame. If using a gas or charcoal grill, preheat a large cast iron skillet over medium-low heat.
2. Evenly distribute the cooled potatoes on a metal sheet tray, drizzle with olive oil, and use a potato masher or small metal bowl to gently smash each potato to a height of about 1/4 to 1/2 inch (thinner potatoes will be crispier).
3. Mix together the butter and garlic. Brush the mixture over each potato, then season with salt and pepper.
4. Pour vegetable oil on griddle, then add flattened potatoes. Cook for 3 minutes, then flip and sprinkle with half of Parmesan. Cook for 3 minutes, then flip, sprinkle with remaining Parmesan, and cook 1 minute.
5. Transfer to a pan, sprinkle with parsley and serve hot.

Conclusion

Any meals of the day is included, no matter what you prefer, you will surely find a recipe here easily. Follow this cookbook with straightforward instructions, encouraging advice, and you will save more time and money cooking delicious food.

There are various books available in the market on this topic, thanks for choosing my cookbook. I hope you love and enjoy all the recipes written in this cookbook.

www.ingramcontent.com/pod-product-compliance
Lightning Source LLC
Chambersburg PA
CBHW081405070526
44583CB00020B/2690